Perhaps It Was Not Mars

Selected Poems

by

Daniel Thomas Moran

ISBN: 978-81-19654-71-0

First Edition: 2024
Rs. 200/-

Cyberwit.net
HIG 45 Kaushambi Kunj, Kalindipuram
Allahabad - 211011 (U.P.) India
http://www.cyberwit.net
Tel: +(91) 9415091004
E-mail: info@cyberwit.net

Printed at Repro India Limited.

For all the many teachers I had and the ones I did not.

And always... for Karen

Acknowledgements

Some of the poems in this collection were first published in the following journals and magazines:

Ars Poetica, Confrontation, Exit 13, Freefall, Humanist Network News, The Poet's Touchstone, iManhattan, Mobius, Mojo Risin', Nassau Review, Newsday, Northport Arts Magazine, Poetry Salzburg Review,Poetry tREnD Anthology, Poets Choice/At Central Park Anthology, Street Magazine, The Seventh Quarry,

Contents

Perhaps It Was Not Mars

Lord of all conflict,
outstanding upon
the new darkness
that July night,
subtle but certain
in that field of stars.

Our eyes led
by a way of light
to the profile
of a waxing moon.

Perhaps Saturn
who plants faith,
or Jupiter whose
dominance moves
the thunder and skies.
It did not matter.

It was all
there before us,
nameless and ancient,
those million million
pinholes in
the drape of night.

The slender moon
left scents for me
in the shadows
on your tender neck.

Until morning,
it was Mercury
god of eloquence,
and Venus ascending
again and again.

Things Past

There
are times
when I wish
that I could weep
out loud for
all of them

But
I know
too well that
the future will
not stop to
allow me

No
more than
a pane of
glass would allow
but one breath
to pass through.

Inspiration

Often, in
the violet evening
I sit waiting,
for the hum of
gyros and whirligigs
inside my egg-shell
skull to resume my
living, to raise up
a fresh font from
a dry place.

Some of
my children live
on pages which,
on windless nights,
I rustle in my
fingertips to emulate
the absent breeze.

I say
to them
listen closely,
for the footsteps
of the zephyr are
easy to miss in this
un-consoling dark.

Illusions

Have my

illusions

and I will

have yours

Evading

the light

like

two mice

With

the plans

to

the house

On Fifth Avenue

Saint Patrick's
sends jeweled spires
into the wide skyline,
close to imagined heaven
as faith itself,

Its prodigious crown
set hard upon chiseled
marble colonnades,
huge as the thighs of
some almighty God.

For brief moments
each day, sunlight
lances the stained-glass
spilling vivid rivulets
over oak and goldleaf,
stone and flesh,

A canyon so hollow, a
single splash of tear will
echo among the rafters,
nearly to the ears of
the auricle himself.

At the rear vestibule,
before the tarnished and
towering bronze doors,
a humble brass box pleads,
For the Poor.

A Five Dollar Poem

I warn you,
this is a bad poem.
Sentimental.
Self-indulgent.
And full of shit.
Dripping with
sugar and acidity.

Its lines bounce
like a cube upon
a bed of nails.
Its rhymes strain
the limits of plausibility.

The meaning
of this poem will be
obscure a crow in
black walnut tree on
a moonless night.
Tomorrow I will wish
I had never thought
to compose it.

Then, I will humbly
preface it with a simple
Dear Editor, and
fatuously hope it will
be lauded as genius,
so that one shining day

I might assume my place
as a prized pillar in
the temple of verse.

For Allen Planz

Your brain lies
suspended on stilts
above Sablowski's garage.

Through the blue
lace of stale smoke,
the bay's docks
beckon you down
to the swinging tides,
beyond the horizon
to the realms of
cod and yellow fin.

Over your roof
floats the halo of
thermonuclear poetics,
drowning the constellations,
and the plaintive reflections
of a captive moon.

Harlem Sunday Afternoon

Up here,
the city has
not changed for
a hundred years.

The resonant blues
hang like crepe
over the geometry
of tenement rows,

The percussive call
of woeful anger
pounding against
defiled glass and
crumbling brick.

On the corner
of Martin Luther King
and Malcolm X Boulevards,
at the vortex of despair,
a most splendid lady,

Head to toe in her
Sunday meeting best,
ivory wool, ivory leather,
a grand ivory fascinator.

She was pride and jazz
and angel dignity,

Eyes lit and aloft, gazing
high above the ruins,

Within the gray commotion,
serenaded by angels,
and invisible to all
but the poets.

A Monarch in Alphabet City

Above Second Avenue,
the butterfly was
tossed about
in the din, and
the filthy updraft
of buses and
yellow taxis
as they raced
thru the long
asphalt valleys.

Exhausted and dis-
oriented it alighted
and queried a
soft-faced passerby.
Pardon me friend,
which way to Mexico?

The passerby
could only shrug
and say
he had no idea,
It must be up
in the Bronx.

Anopheles

You watch me
from some
invisible toe-hold
in a distant corner
of my room,

Patient as
an undertaker
on a foggy
New Year's Eve.

To you,
I must seem
beautiful
in my furless,
featherless repose,

A prodigious ocean
from which you
are desiring but
one small sip.

Never Cross a Woman

There she came,
as if from nowhere,
Betty Friedan-
mother of all women,
the feminine mystic
lobbying justice with
an upraised fist,
high priestess of
uterine actualization.

There she came in
a rusty old Plymouth,
daring as she must to
navigate the tight spots,
careening off of
the nice lady's
new Beemer in the
noontime bedlam of
a Sag Harbor summer,
and stepped out
to the confrontation.

The nice lady said,
Save the speech Betty.
Who's going to pay
for this goddamned
crease in my door?
When my husband
sees this, he is going
to kill me.

The Sisters of Mercy

The nuns
taught us that
mute obedience,
dogma, and shame
are a boy's best friend.

Suffering in their
dark eternities,
cloistered in the
mildew that lives
within their
stony walls.

Haunted faces
framed in stiff,
virginal linen,
breastless and hairless,
stripped of womanhood,
motherhood, and lust.

In this way, they
apply their vengeance,
wooden rulers
extracting the dignity
from tiny white knuckles.

We, always fearing,
as witless sinners
on the jagged road

road to condemnation,
just what their god
was concealing beneath
those black habits.

After Three Children

Some days,
I awaken
like a sailor
on a weekend
shore leave,
a strange woman
lying beside me,
and a large
three-headed dragon
freshly tattooed
on my chest,
uncertain just
what the hell
had happened.

Awaiting Creation

On this night
anticipating summer,
there is only
the dark and its
spare silence,
the murmurs
of creatures are
woven well thru it.

Into my
open window,
the echoes of
a thundering in
the near distance,
the occasional
flash confused
with blinking.

I await the
overture to follow
the tuning of strings.
But the budding
tempest, favoring
a northward course,
grants no wind, no
rain, no cataclysm.

At times, creation
can feel that near,
At times, just that
far away.

On Loving, Leaving, Television and Prosperity

When I divorced
my first wife,
she got our daughter
and the T.V.

When I married
my second wife,
she had her
own TV, but
let my daughter
and me look at it.

When I finished
paying off
my first wife
for having been
married to me,
my second wife
had money for TV's
and she bought them.

When I divorced
my second wife,
she got our
daughter and son
and all the TV's.

When I moved into
the bachelor bungalow,

I bought myself
a nice clock radio,
so I might be reminded
to get out of my bed
each day, to
work and earn money,
so I could finish
paying off
my second wife,
for having been
married to me.

When my first wife
got word of it,
she felt badly, and
offered her old TV,
certain I was languishing
before the radio's
prosaic green digits
without The Simpsons,
or Seinfeld, or
Monday Night Football.

I declined in fear
I might look at it,
choosing rather
to simply contemplate
over the Public Radio
purr, just who might
love a man with
two wives, three children,
and no TV.

Eleven Couplets

The most gifted of mornings
comes to coax the eyes from sleep,

The pleadings from feathered breast
through the length of early shadows,

The stars expiring, exhaling breath
one by one by one.

Somewhere, something mourns
the slow dying of the darkness.

It is ever thus with this world,
spinning certain and silent,

A bearing in the great machine,
the perfect precious chaos.

And so it is too
with this loving of ours.

In a universe deep and unbounded
which abhors the constant,

Which seeks to make an elliptical path
through the cold ethers of time,

Daring to show its blue countenance
to the expressionless firmament,

What peace might we seek, what solace,
than to believe we are not alone.

Sex Education

LEVEL ONE:

Child:

Daddy,
were you there
when they
took me
out of
Mommy's belly?

Father:

I sure was.
By the way,
what were
you doing
in there?

Child:

I don't know.

PROCEED TO LEVEL TWO:

The New Testament

Jesus was a poet,
arriving at weddings
armed with lies and
a bottle of cheap wine.

Never letting the dead
rest easy in their sleep,
he allowed the academics
to strip off his robes
and drive nails through
his hands and feet.

He left behind
his silly sycophants
to spend eternity
repairing the holes
in their nets.

He walked nimbly
over the water simply
because he had never
been taught to swim.

His poems were
prayers to the deaf sky,
words scratched onto
a child's paper chain.

Jesus was a poet,
and like the poet,
no wiser than
the man who
goes to the well to
gape into his reflection
and quench his thirst.

To An Irish Poet

Your words arose like
the slow pale foam rising
from a bog-colored stout
and circled round me,
sharp as a whistle in
an empty dance hall.
The far distant blue
in your eyes, those of
a brother I never knew.

I spoke of the
gentle exhuming of my
long-expired relations,
my earnest desires to carry
what remains of their
chalky, splintered bones,

Back and back to where
seabirds pirouette and plunge
and rise again on the salted wind,
High above the hardened ledges
of the westward coasts where the
wet cloak of the brackish air
smells of recognition and toil.

You spoke of young evenings
where the dark birthed dreams
of steamships, your feet longing
for those American highways
far beyond your tufted hills.

I conjure the ghosts of wood ships,
masts leaning westward to where
dawn lifts the lace skirts of morning.
Willing, like the Jack of our fables
traveling the perilous path to town,
to surrender my coins for a fistful
of magic.

Water

The

summer sun
sucks the moisture
from my zillion pores,

Up

to heaven, I suppose,
to be used to
water lawns, feed
rivers and waterfalls,
and quench the seas.

One

drop at a time, trickling
down from my brow,
and thru the subtle valleys
of my back,

Then

up to the clouds
for a trip round this
grand blue planet,

Finally

parachuting back to
the Earth, making
the tiniest splash
and ripple in a
muddy puddle in Peking.

Ascendency

for Samuel Menashe

His eye is
upon the sparrow,

But the sparrow
has no clue.

The sparrow,
unlike The Almighty,

has more important
things to do.

Concerning Ants

Never say can't
to any ant,
for you can trust
his work is a must.

Don't waste words dissuading,
his living's parading.
He's abandoned his will
to exist for his hill.

Never say never,
the ant is too clever.
Don't waste your time asking
if satisfaction his tasks bring.

No antipathies lurking
for he's too busy working.
Whether lugging or linking,
he can't be bothered with thinking.

Not a moment for fretting
about any giving and getting.
You will not hear him ranting
about his life anting.

The language of ant
does not include can't.

From Saint Farnan's Well

for Yvonne Henry

I've been down to Ballymeeny,
to speak with the wind
and the dead, beside a
smooth swale of shore
which slid like a penstroke
away from Ben Bulben.

I stood at the top of
a lane rutted by rain and
the farmer's wood wheels,
humbled by a horizon
which birthed the days.
Against a sky of rare cyan
clouds tumbled like
cream into steaming tea.

I looked to the glen where
a freshet slid from the hills.
I looked for you, Delia Kilcullen,
filling a drowsy bucket at
St. Farnan's well, your feet,
like mine, wet with the mud.

I looked for your brothers,
and your father calling for
the strayed lamb, your mother

under the brittle thatch
feeding turf to the fire.

They were all so young,
and you but a maiden when
you left them, wild and unsettled
as the knotted briar among
these scattered stones.

A girl who knew, not far
beyond this darkened door, lived
all the desires that ever were.

You listened in twilight to the
thunder of a tides never stilled.
With your bucket at each daybreak,
you imagined distant cities, the sun
lifting the green hem of the sea.

Scriptures

Of all to be said
of gods and men

Drawing truth from a
sharpened quill

Are the many ways
they write of love

And the ease with which
they kill

The Sailboat Pond

Central Park in April

A coursing of clouds contain
the expectant glint of April sun.

Pastels and greens of life reborn
from the heights of knotted trees,
speckle the skin of the murky pond,
imposing towers standing sentinel.

Hans Andersen poses on a pedestal.
Alice perches upon a toadstool.
Slight birds speak from chance perches,
searching for sustenance from
among the crumbs of men.

I sit grasping pen and yellow scrap,
sharing space in the ring of bench,
contemplating heaven and center
as if something could soon happen.

But there is only a child's calling,
the muted mutter of a passerby,
a silence straining against itself
and a dapple of gray and light,

On a pond which cradles the sky in
a land of fairytales and new blossoms,
and tiny boats drifting in an almost
absent breeze to nowhere at all.

The Swimming Lesson

Down at the tired shores
of Florence Ave. Beach,
an optimist in green trunks
was instructing us on
how to become swimmers.

We, a dozen or so
scrawny specimens on
an early summer day,
one o'clock sharp,
up to our tiny thighs
in that oily chill.

We knew there
were secrets, that things
lived beneath it all.
We knew, as we stood,
within minutes
the sandy bottom
would swallow our feet.
Our young mothers
looked on from old blankets,
proud for unknown reasons.

Then the instructor said,
with great authority,
First thing we'll learn
is the dead man's float.

Some cried but most tried,
facing down into
the briny darkness.

We let the bubbles rise
back across our cheeks,
and we made believe we
had failed to learn to swim.

The Horseshoe Crabs Mating along Delaware Bay

That old horseshoe crab, among
the oddest of odd creatures,
defies those instinctively
fond of fine features.

Neither crab nor horse,
you cannot eat or shoe them,
and when seen on their back
there ain't too much to them.

Tumbling in love in the surf,
you might think that they'll botch it,
but as the dinosaurs went extinct,
they were right there to watch it.

Walking Central Park at Dusk

In the captured divinity
of this lush and rolling paradise,

one Olmsted witnessed,
lost deep in perfect sleep,

with our fingers woven, our
steps have found their meter.

Enjoined in the sway
of this gentle strolling,

following a path beside ponds
which blacken beneath willows,

definition retires in deference
to the rising nightfall.

Extinguishing just beyond seeing,
a necklace of lamp posts,

stars perching on pedestals.
They stand erect and elegant,

illuminating our way home.

New York to Boston

How odd this life, coming
toward a new wonder. Now
of two score and ten years,
hair growing ashen, my frame
bending toward slowing steps.
A whole life of reaching, of
touching each thing, small and large
if only to be touched.

From my suckling moment
I have straddled this island,
caught between oceans and sounds
between what was and might be.
I have loved this roiling city,
the hardness of its streets,
the tumult, the stench and
the sounds of singing
from men and machines too.

I have been to the harbor of New York.
I have seen the ships berth and set off,
listened to the creaking of masts, witnessed
the disembarking of hope onto the piers.
I have watched the faces and gaits
of those who emerged, if only
to find my own and be found.

I have seen the struggle and
I have struggled as well, known

the pains of the heart-torn,
looked up to see things
far too mighty to fathom.
I've seen tiny flowers spring
from concrete, and leaves
which fell onto the mountains,
finding their way to the sea.

And, I have hoped, like
every fool, to live forever,
not imagining fatigue might
visit upon such notions.
I have failed at love
and it has failed me as well,
my children grown, slowly gone,
all mothers long gone,
people unfamiliar and distant,
now familiar and at hand.

Birds stab at seeds I have left,
growing yellow like spring.
Cats walk over my bed at morning,
content to be alone together.

I have been awed by
moments and matters I cannot now recall,
seeking the familiar in foreign countries,
where my ancestors kneeled and prayed
beneath white clapboard and steeples,
never considering that heaven was empty.
I have come to contain my living
within brick walls, walking brick paths.

There is finally a place where
I can be no one to everyone,
where no one calls to ask
and I ask nothing, where it is
only love and my lover and me,
living at the top and bottom
of fourteen hardwood steps,
looking out at the South End streets
through a dozen tall panes of glass.
We hear the sounds cities make
and attempt our harmony.

Friends old and growing old,
we too old and growing older.
It is the right time for it.
To grow old, to be old
and soon enough be done
with being both young and old.
We will get there in good time,
gone when it is no longer our time.

For now, from within the confines
of this city, perched on seven hills,
there is a morning at my window that
warms the bedding which contains us.
People are on the streets, ships first
emptying, then filling the decayed docks
of this new and ancient harbor.

The sparrow who lives
at a corner near our window
is busy reminding us of all

we will need to know,
to build the nest well, make
the best of this day as we have it.
Spring was fleeting and summer too.

Beep

Our new automatic rice
cooker sings to us when
we turn it on.
Our dishwasher sings
when it turns off.

The clothes dryer
declaims in a voice that is
decidedly more aggressive.
It points a gun at our head, and
demands to be emptied. Now.
The laptop, a real free spirit,
chortles all day long for
any number of reasons.

But it is the car I hate,
the car that reminds me of
a wife left behind years ago.
It nags and nags and nags again
with buzzes and beeps and dings,
apprising me of my failures.

Forgetting to latch
my safety belt, not shutting
the door all the way, over-
looking an overdue oil change.

It especially loves to let me know
(with an unmistakable glee), that

I've been driving quite long enough
with my turn signal going, all
the other drivers having
already called me an idiot.

I don't mind the chirps that
tell me I am about to be run
down by a truck backing up,
or the one that clicks to tell
blind people that they can
now safely cross the street.

Even my new hearing aids,
that make it possible for me
to hear all the other electronic things
that niggle and afflict me, feel
they must bleat their tiny melody
straight into my ear when their
battery is about to die.
If they did not, I might not
ever hear all the other beeps,
and jingles and cheerful tinkles.
Would that not be tragically delicious,
especially when served up with
perfectly cooked rice?

Fundamentals

When they say bad things
about the flock,
It makes us want
to fling a rock.

When someone's mean
to our messiah,
It makes us want
to burn a tire.

When our god's the
punch-line of a joke,
It's time to fill the streets
with smoke.

When we're subjected to
a verbal shiv,
Let's destroy the places
where we live.

The gods and prophets
we're loudly praising,
Will bless us for this
Hell we're raising.

One For Dear O'Brien

My cup is filled,
my elbow bent,
to Hell with the light bill
and the rent.

Place a splash of Red Breast
beside my Stout,
offer us up a toast
that sounds devout.

To great St. Patrick
and Hissoner too,
to the boys of Eire
that are wearing blue.

To the Irish who
built this bloody town,
from Sligo and Mayo
and the County Down.

The day's been long,
but the publican's buying,
so let's raise up a glass
to Dear O'Brien.

As We Fall Asleep

I am
the
teacup.

Against
me,
you round

yourself,
and
then hang

your legs
over
the rim.

In The Dark

There are always those things which
should have been said but were not,
things withheld and thoughts
chased like crows from the garden.

It is not always what is seen,
or even what is not seen,
maybe what we'd rather not see.

The face can betray the heart,
the seeming to manage even
with a world inside in chaos.

Who can ever know another,
when we are all only children
hiding behind the parlor drape,
covering our tiny eyes to be
safe from the monsters.

It may be necessary in this life
for some things to end badly,
questions to never be answered.
Things do end so very badly at times.

Questions persist and persist
and haunt even our dreaming.
We take them with us, into
the dark and the sleep, yet
they always awake with us.

Even as we wander the world,
nomads in search of found places,
they know where we are going
and they stay close behind.

The Haiku Poet

All of the verse
he ever wrote

he penned within
a Post-it Note.

Asserting, "There must
be things far worse

than poems square
and pale and terse".

Sons and Fathers

In their odd hats and coats,
they practice to be their own fathers.

In their hard-soled shoes,
they desire to be a definition.

They understand what might have been,
and then never was,

Driven by an undefined madness,
to do what must be done.

In the pale breath of swelling moonlight,
their children cradled by the darkness,

They seem to be near but,
they might be anywhere else.

If you live long enough,
you too, will come to claim it.

The table set without chairs,
the awareness shared in our descent.

And in our falling life, everything
will seem taller than it was, yet

Never so tall as it needed to be.

On Tranquility

after Robert Frost

Is there the thing
so sublime, so rare,
Might I find the
perfect silence there?

Of moment and measure
forever bound,
To a place of none
but the gentlest sound.

Where our whispers
might lie upon the quiet,
Where even the light
could not defile it.

No belief would ever
require disproving,
A single leaf to speak
that the airs are moving.

Content possessing,
no ache of longing,
Through noon and gloom
through night to dawning.

Sonnet for the Oak Moon

Moon over our midnight
like a giant's heart,
Bids that darkness from
our bare trees depart.

How generous
this peculiar thing,
That brings a noon to this
benumbed evening.

Your striking light
so much rarer yet,
Than all the lesser stars
we may for now forget.

Late wakened on this night
we will long recall,
We paid morning's sun
no mind at all.

The only thing in your light,
as yet unclear.
What of this night, dear Moon,
drew you so near?

The Man from an Unknown Place

Along the waterfront
in Old Bombay,
beside the
Gateway of India,

Stood a man dressed
in a black kurta pajama,
who asked where
I was from.

I said Boston, and
he said he
had never heard
of it.

I said, How
about New York?
He just said,
"No."

A Gold Case in Paris

I have a gold watch,
bought in *Ile de la Cite*
on my last *lune de miel.*

It runs well, but
twenty-three minutes
fast every day.

I look at it, but I
never know what time
it might really be.

It is always
sometime
just prior.

Like me, my wife
loves the watch,
just as she loved Paris.

She often tells me
that she loves
me as well, except

For my always
being early, thinking
I am right on time.

The Man Who First Lived in This House

The man who first
lived in this house
painted the shingles red.
He left a steel pulley
over a rafter in the garage
on which he hung
his old outboard motors.

In the corner of the footing
he used a stick to mark "1964"
in the wet concrete. After that,
I'll bet his car never suffered
another night in the rain.

There was a horse shoe
nailed over the back door
which I don't dare remove.
But there was never a horse,

Just three cats, who
lived long lives or did not,
whom he buried beneath
markers of one by two pine,
their tiny names effaced by sun
and many years of rainy days.

Whatever remains of them
shares the corner of the yard
with an old hand pump, its

one arm seized forever in rust,
which has not expressed
a drop of water in decades.

There was a woman too, but
a woman I don't care to talk about.
She had many acquaintances
but no friends, and a crazy son who
either ran away or was chased.

The best to be said of her was that
she swam in the bay right through November,
and that she collected scraps of meat
to feed the sad cats at the dump.

But she was hard and nasty as something
you might stub a toe against in the dark.
Sometimes people like that
can live forever, and she almost did.
Their husbands often die young,
of passing the hours in the garage
piecing together old boat motors and
thinking of bluefish and little neck clams.

The woman who lives here with me,
does not swim or search for scraps.
I am often found sitting in this chair
wondering what cats think about,
tucked into a windowsill watching
brown leaves falling on the grass,
and deer wandering among the trees
with no place more special to be.

I have tried my best to stay out of boats,
and to love the secret of the waters
from a dry purchase on the shore.
Near the hanging steel pulley there is
a workbench the man left behind,
where he made crucifixes for cats and
attempted to fix all the broken things.

I too have work to be done, but not there.
I only need a stylus and a sheaf like this one,
and the desire to see the world through
the eyes of a cat or a man with a steel pulley.

The Task

All of her life
she was probably
one of those people
to whom you
could give a task
and know it
would be done.

There are so
very few like that
in this life.
They are rare
as blue moons
or redheaded babies.

They are the
people of whom
you can ask anything,
look the other way,
and when you
turn back again the
numbers are summed.

She was one
of those people
who always knew
how to gather
all that they would
need to know.

On a morning in August,
she set her watch
to the kitchen clock,
making sure to
latch the back door.

In the room,
within a long hallway
at a hotel for
weary travelers,
she opened the book
one more time, just
to be sure that
she had it right.

She let the great
weight of her head
make a last impression
in the center of the pillow.

The amber bottle emptied,
her task accomplished,
she closed her eyes
and left us all behind.

To The Academy

The poet professors
who have to teach,
Say poetry's a prominence
beyond mortal reach.

While the anointed reign,
I will, contented, deign,
Not bent on the brilliance,
my betters feign.

Contented burrowing
beneath the breach,
They calculate the sands,
where I see a beach.

Ode To Dame Edna

Dame Edna just
loved to impress us,
With her baubles
and lavender tresses.
What we could neither
imagine nor see,
Was that she so typ-
ically stood to pee,
And had flies sewn
into all of her dresses.

Aeroporto Leonardo DaVinci

Roma, Italia 27 Oct 2011

We are all marooned
in Rome, at the airport
named for Leonardo DaVinci,
Trying to get
back to Boston before
that long winter has us
in its merciless clutches.

The Italians tell us
that the plane is broken,
that they must either fix it
or get another.
Thus far, here on this
late October day in Rome,
they seem able to do neither.

And so we are trapped,
all of us now together.
A little blue nun.
A young girl with a book.
Twenty-seven grieving
Italian widows.
A half dozen decrepit souls
plopped in airport wheelchairs.
Any number of lumpy Italian
women wearing leopard undies.

Three hotheaded cannolis
expressing their frustrations
with flying hands.
Eighteen old men
in shorts their wives
made them wear so
that they will look relaxed
on this holiday they planned
back when the kids were small.

None of us are happy.
None of us want to hear
the newest excuse from the
pretty attendants in green skirts.

We want only to be
where we are going.
Someplace far from here,

Where people think only
of Leonardo DaVinci as
that incomparable old
maestro mago genio
that he was back when,

Sitting quietly alone,
musing upon a gentle hillside
near the ancient trees
thick with ripening olives,
gazing long and longingly
at the deep blue Italian sky,

Wondering what if?
What if only men could fly?

Once Home

for Annie Henry nee Kilcullen

Settled against
a trough in a hillside,
the narrow arched
doorway led southward,
backed against the sea
and shell-strewn shore.

Would it have been
your father or his who
collected and carried
each jagged stone?
Who laid them edge to
edge, corner to crenel,
until they were composed
just tall enough to contain
the height of a man?

Once a roof of crisp thatch
angled to banish
the wind and pelting rain,
it has finally succumbed to
the vagaries of day and sky.
Walls once sure, now
downed and crumbled, a
byre for another man's cows.

Now, they and we
stand overtaken by bog iris,
new daisies and fodder.
The great struggles and small,
the turning seasons, the fiddling
and stepping long-ended.

What is gone after all?
Not your name.
Not the leaning Ben Bulben.
Neither the river nor sky.
Not the serenity beside this rill.
And surely not the sea,
the ancient incessant sea.

The Dusts of Pompeii

17Oct11 at the Bay of Napoli on The Queen Victoria

The dusts of Pompeii
are upon my feet,
captured time
in fine ash.

Jupiter's stone columns
against the cerulean sky,
ever upright as they
were that last day.

Rooms where children
slept among distant dreams.
Hearths where the baker
turned straw to
flour, flour to gold.
Sailors straddled the shore,
drank full, and reclined into
the arms of harlots.

Once, April rains fell
through the rutted stone,
faltering to the primeval sea.
Once, Apollo poured sunlight
over the hillsides.

Here is this day, just
as in some once-long-ago,
beside the tranquil Vesuvius,
maker of quakes and tombs.

The Master Makes a Line

My youth made
dancers move.
The curtain up,
beauty and poise
spinning within
the purple shades
of candles.

With my oils,
I made them delicate
and strong, possessed of
inexhaustible youth.

Then there were
the ladies,
hundreds of them,
each one anxious
to recline before me.

Now I sit,
captured in this room,
betrayed by clocks,
legs all but useless,
hands twisted as knots.

I must ask
my young girl
to strap a stick
to my arm, and

coax open the
bottle of ink.

I will show her
how it can be,
that a man can still
possess his gift.

That even
a single line,
can become
a miracle.

Attente

The
less-
ons
of
pat-

ience

Are
lea-
rned
slow-
ly.

The Galapagos Islands

Nov 2012

Here in Black Turtle Cove,
the morning's waters are
low and smooth,

Broken only by the soft
stroking of Julio's white paddle
at the panga's ropey prow.

It draws us forward, into
the angling sunrise,
closer to the mangrove,
dense green against sharp light,

Suspended by a woven nest
of gnarled woods,
lying like a garland against
the water's edge.

Here on the island called Santa Cruz,
the ancient sacred turtles cross
from the South Pacific into the
blue-emerald shallows.

They are willed here by that force,
which adjures them to
the godless eternal, and
calls them to the dance of life.

When Nothing Happens

I have stared out
through this window before.
Many times.
Who knows
the sums of such things?

I was there this morning,
a fresh mug of coffee
sending the aroma of waking
up from the table beside me.

Yesterday, the trees
were the waving arms
of children at a parade.
The sunrise was
a golden flood.

In winter, the finches
were the ghosts of spring.
The frozen pond
a tomb for the sky.

The Christmas cactus was
the ebon night above us
on the Fourth of July, and
the hill which lifts this house
fell away from the porch
like the falter toward eternity.

But on this day,
the glass is only glass.
The rain is only the rain.
This morning is but the
last of last night.
The cats are just cats.
The leaves of the laurel
look as they do, and

I am only a man
in an old robe,
cradling a cooled cup,
capped pen in his pocket,
and likely to be late
for work.

www.ingramcontent.com/pod-product-compliance
Lightning Source LLC
Chambersburg PA
CBHW022202160726
48282CB00024B/286
9788119654710